All rights reserved.

First published in this format 2014

Text and Patterns: Linda Zemba Burhance
Jacket/Cover and Interior Design: Kimberly Adis
Photographer: Alexandra Grablewski
Executive Editor, Series: Shawna Mullen
Assistant Editor, Series: Timothy Stobierski
Series Art Director: Rosalind Loeb Wanke
Series Production Editor: Lynne Phillips
Series Copy Editor: Barbara Cottingham

The Taunton Press
Inspiration for hands-on living®

The Taunton Press, Inc., 63 South Main Street,
PO Box 5506, Newtown, CT 06470-5506
e-mail: tp@taunton.com

Threads® is a trademark of The Taunton Press, Inc.,
registered in the U.S. Patent and Trademark Office.

The following names/manufacturers appearing in
Arm Knitting are trademarks: Bernat®,
Harry Potter[SM], Lion®, Loops & Threads®,
Premier®, Red Heart®

Library of Congress Cataloging-in-Publication Data
in progress

ISBN: 978-1-62710-886-7

Printed in the United States of America
10 9 8 7 6 5 4 3 2 1

CONTENTS

14
FUN TIMES INFINITY SCARF

16
ANIMAL INSTINCT FABRIC SCARF

18
SUPER COZY THROW

26
SOFT & CUDDLY BLANKET

28
GREEN GODDESS CAPE

30
TURQUOISE FANTASY COLLARED CAPELET

INTRODUCTION

**Arm knitting is so much fun! And the best part is:
You can do it, even if you don't know how to knit!**

I RECENTLY TAUGHT A group of people at a major yarn expo in New York City, and the range of skill went from expert knitter to knitting novice. I am happy to say that after a few simple demonstrations of casting on, arm knitting, and casting off, everyone was knitting, even the "non" knitters.

You will amaze and delight your friends with this simple technique. With arm knitting, you are the designer! Get your creative juices flowing by combining different yarns to create your own spectacular works of art.

There are three basic things to know before you begin:

1. Size Doesn't Matter. Unlike knitting with needles, there is no standard arm size. Everyone's arms are different, so you will get your own custom results. You don't have to worry about needle size and gauge, so it is a very stress-free form of knitting.

2. Lefty or Righty, You Can Arm Knit. Unlike traditional knitting, there isn't a left-handed or a right-handed way of arm knitting. It's the same for everyone. With arm knitting, you use both arms and both hands equally, so the technique is universal. And you don't need to know how to knit in order to arm knit: Just follow the simple steps and pictures provided for casting on, knitting back and forth, and casting off, and you're done!

3. You're the Designer. This is the best kept secret of arm knitting: You can use just about any yarn combination to create a beautiful new accessory! It's a great way to combine yarns to make a version that appeals to you. And if you happen to have a yarn stash that is taking over the guest room, the closet, and the attic, you can use that too! Try combining novelty with bulky or chenille with eyelash, for example. It's entirely up to you. The sky is the limit!

The following patterns indicate a measurement based on my arms, but you can knit until you have the measurement that works best for you. I hope you find arm knitting as irresistible as I do!

CASTING ON

This type of casting on is called a **Long Tail Cast On**. Arm knitting always involves using multiple strands of yarn at once. Here I am using six strands of yarn, but you will use however many strands are specified in your project.

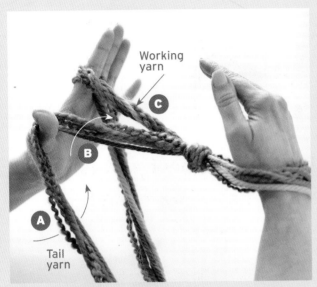

1. Make a slip knot and put it on your right hand. Wrap the working yarn (yarn coming off of the skein) around your pointer finger, and the tail yarn (yarn closest to your body) around your thumb as shown. With your right hand, go under the tail yarn **(A)**, over strands **(B)**, and grasp the working yarn **(C)**.

2. Pull the yarn that you've just grasped up to make a loop. Then let go with your left hand.

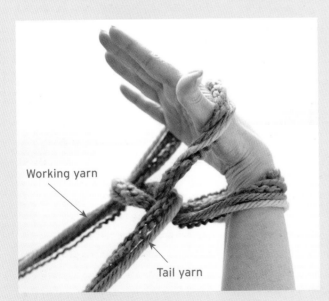

3. Put the newly created loop (stitch) onto your right hand. Lightly tighten, but be sure that the stitch is not too tight.

4. You now have two stitches cast on. Repeat steps 1 through 3 creating stitches on your right hand until you have the number of stitches called for in your pattern.

ARM KNITTING

As Easy as One, Two, Three!

1. Hold the working yarn in your right hand. Grasp a stitch in your left hand.

2. Pull the stitch over your working yarn.

3. Place the new stitch on the left arm, and repeat until all stitches are on left arm!

Now Go Back the Other Way!

4. Hold the working yarn in your left hand. Grasp a stitch in your right hand.

5. Pull the stitch over your working yarn.

6. Place the new stitch on the right arm, and repeat until all stitches are on right arm!

KNIT TWO TOGETHER

Some arm knitting projects use a special stitch called **"Knitting two stitches together"** (K2TOG in knitting lingo) and it's much easier than you might think. Simply hold two stitches together and pull the working yarn through both stitches at the same time as if they are one stitch, and you end up with just one stitch! This effectively removes a stitch from your row, and as such is great for projects that need to curve or angle.

CASTING OFF

For all of these projects you will always end your knitting with the stitches on your left arm. Now, you are ready to finish your project by casting off. Here's how.

1. Knit two stitches onto your right hand.

2. Pull the first stitch over the second stitch and let go. Your stitches should remain fairly loose.

3. Keep knitting one stitch at a time and pulling the previous stitch over the one you just knit until you have none left! It's super easy!

4. Now that you've completed your work, all you have to do is weave your ends in and you are done!

YOUR TEAM
RIBBON INFINITY SCARF

Show your team or school spirit! You'll look fabulous for the big game—all you need is yarn and your hands! No needles, no stress. In no time at all you'll be showing your true colors! GO TEAM!

SKILL LEVEL
Beginner

FINISHED MEASUREMENTS
60" long before connecting ends

6" wide

YARN
3 skeins team colors ribbon yarn (CYCA 6)

SHOWN IN
Red Heart® Boutique Sashay Team Spirit in Purple/Gold

NOTIONS (OPTIONAL)
Crochet hook for weaving in yarn ends

Needle and thread to stabilize the ends for a more finished look

To Make Scarf

1. Holding three strands together, cast on 4 stitches, as shown on p. 5.
You may want to make sure the yarn starts at a different place on each skein to truly mix up the color!

2. Knit each row as shown on p. 6. Continue the process until you reach your desired length of 27 rows or approximately 60". Due to the nature of arm knitting, these are approximate measurements; just make sure you can wrap it twice around your neck!

3. Cast off, as shown on p. 7.

Finishing

Once you have cast off, just place the ends together and weave the ribbon tail through the knit and tie off to link the two sides together making an infinity scarf. You can use your hands or a crochet hook to weave the yarn tails in.

VARIATION Make a scarf for every team in your life: football, baseball, high school, college, favorite Harry Potter℠ house—the combinations are endless!

TIP

Due to the loose nature of arm knitting, use a needle and thread to sew the ribbon yarn to itself once the ends are woven in. This stabilizes the ends so they don't work their way back out—you don't want it falling apart.

POM POM PRETTY
SCARF

This scarf is super easy and quick to make. And the pom poms are already attached to the yarn, so what could be easier? Best of all: You'll have made it yourself!

SKILL LEVEL
Beginner

FINISHED MEASUREMENTS
96" long
12" wide

YARN
2 skeins Chenille Super Bulky Yarn (CYCA 6)

1 skein Chenille Super Bulky Novelty Yarn with pre-attached Pom Poms (CYCA 6)

SHOWN IN
Red Heart Boutique Chic in Blush

Bernat® Baby Blanket in Peachy

NOTIONS (OPTIONAL)
Needle and thread to stabilize the ends for a more finished look

To Make Scarf

1. Holding three strands together, cast on 5 stitches, as shown on p. 5.

Reserve two pom poms with 6" of yarn on both sides of each pom pom to add to the ends of your finished scarf.

2. Knit each row as shown on p. 6. Continue the process until you reach your desired length of 41 rows or approximately 96".

3. Cast off, as shown on p. 7.

Finishing

Tie the corners together on each of the short ends. Using ends, attach your reserved length of pom pom yarn so that it hangs down from each end of the scarf. Weave in remaining ends. You can use your hands or a crochet hook.

VARIATION You can easily change up the design of this scarf by using pom pom yarns for all of your working strands to get more fun pom poms all over!

TIP

Take care when finishing that your yarn ends are secured. Use a needle and thread to stabilize the ends of the yarn if they are too loose or if you want a more finished look.

TIP

To prevent the braided yarn from unraveling use a needle and thread to join the ends of the yarn to the body of the work, hiding the stitches in the yarn.

KNIT WIT
COWL

The yarn used in this scarf is braided, so it looks like you spent hours, when it only takes a few minutes to complete. Use all of that extra time to make a second one, or go out and rake in the compliments. What a showstopper!

SKILL LEVEL
Beginner

FINISHED MEASUREMENTS
30" long
9" wide

YARN
1 skein Super Bulky Novelty Yarn that looks braided (CYCA 6)

SHOWN IN
Red Heart Boutique Dash in Meadow

NOTIONS (OPTIONAL)
Needle and thread to stabilize the ends for a more finished look

To Make Scarf

1. Cast on 7 stitches, as shown on p. 5.

The stitches in arm knitting are very loose, making it easy for the "loops" to snag and tangle. Remembering to take off your rings, watches, and other jewelry will save a lot of frustration as your project gets under way!

2. Knit each row as shown on p. 6. Continue the process until you reach your desired length of 17 rows or approximately 30".

3. Cast off, as shown on p. 7.

Finishing

Once you have cast off, just place short ends of the work together to form a cowl. Tie the ends together and weave the tails through the knit. Tie off to stabilize the yarn.

VARIATION The scarf shown makes use of soft colors to a mellow, but beautiful, affect. Try using different shades of blue for a nautical theme, or pick your favorite hues from the forest canopy for a brilliant autumn accessory.

TIP

If sewing the strand ends together is too intimidating, you can just tie them into bows!

FUN TIMES
INFINITY SCARF

Show off your fashion sense and look glamorous while doing it. Wearing a scarf made of this furry chenille yarn makes it impossible not to have a fun time!

SKILL LEVEL
Beginner

FINISHED MEASUREMENTS
60" long before connecting ends
6" wide

YARN
2 skeins Furry Chenille Yarn (CYCA 6)

SHOWN IN
Loops & Threads® Fashion Fur in Clowning Around

NOTIONS (OPTIONAL)
Crochet hook for weaving in yarn ends
Needle and thread to stabilize the ends for a more finished look

To Make Scarf

1. Holding two strands together, cast on 5 stitches, as shown on p. 5.

There are many types of "Fashion Fur" on the market, for this pattern, make sure you check that your CYCA number is 6, indicating the bulkiest yarn available!

2. Knit each row as shown on p. 6. Continue the process until you reach your desired length of 25 rows or approximately 60".

3. Cast off, as shown on p. 7.

Finishing

Once you have cast off just place the ends together and weave the tail through the knit and tie off to connect the two sides together making an infinity scarf. You can use your hands or a crochet hook. Use a needle and thread to sew the ends of the yarn strands to each other if they seem too loose.

VARIATION Leave the ends disconnected for a fun boa scarf to wrap around your neck or drape over your shoulders!

ANIMAL INSTINCT FABRIC SCARF

This scarf is made from a precut length of chiffon fabric, proof that you can arm knit just about any type of textile. Go wild!

SKILL LEVEL
Beginner

FINISHED MEASUREMENTS
48" long
6" wide

YARN
Chiffon fabric strip approximately 30 yards long, 2–2½" wide (CYCA 6)

SHOWN IN
1 Card of Red Heart Boutique Sassy Fabric in White Cheetah

NOTIONS (OPTIONAL)
Needle and thread to stabilize the fabric-strip ends

To Make Scarf

1. Cast on 6 stitches, as shown on p. 5.

The fabric strips are less stretchy than yarn, so buy an extra card or length of fabric in case you run out based on your own arm measurements.

2. Knit each row as shown on p. 6. Continue the process until you reach your desired length of 25 rows or approximately 48".

3. Cast off, as shown on p. 7.

Finishing

Weave in remaining ends. You can use your hands or a crochet hook.

VARIATION Use a 30-yard roll of lace for an elegant vintage look!

TIP

If you are proficient at a sewing machine, weave the ends in and then sew them to the body of the work in a hidden location. Otherwise, a few stitches with a needle and thread will work.

SUPER COZY THROW

This throw is so soft and warm, you'll be shocked that it was so easy to make! Just combine a fleece fabric strip yarn with super bulky yarn and you're all set. Or you can use yarn from your stash!

SKILL LEVEL
Beginner

FINISHED MEASUREMENTS
48" long
30" wide

YARN
5 skeins fleece type fabric strip yarn (CYCA 5)
2 skeins Super Bulky yarn (CYCA 6)

SHOWN IN
5 strands Premier® Yarn Cuddle Fleece in Circus (CYCA 5)

2 strands Loops & Threads Zoomba in Cascade (CYCA 6)

NOTIONS (OPTIONAL)
Needle and thread to stabilize the ends for a more finished look

To Make Throw

1. Holding seven strands together, (5 strands of the fleece and 2 strands of the super bulky), cast on 13 stitches, as shown on p. 5.

While you are arm knitting, the work can get heavy. Using a table to support the knitting can really keep your arms from getting tired when working on a heavy project like this one. It really is great exercise though!

2. Knit each row as shown on p. 6. Continue the process until you reach your desired length of 23 rows or approximately 48".

3. Cast off, as shown on p. 7.

Finishing

Weave in remaining ends. You can use your hands or a crochet hook.

VARIATION You can make a beautiful earth-tone throw by substituting 6 strands of super bulky yarn in any combination of browns and reds that catch your eye.

TIP

If you want to adorn the throw with fringe or tassels, you can use the leftover yarn to do so, and attach to the top and bottom of the work on every cast on and cast off stitch.

TIP

Make sure when
finishing that
you weave in and
out as evenly as
possible, because
the connection
point will be very
visible. You want
the garment to
have a tidy look.

PURPLE PASSION
SHRUG

Passionate about knitting? This contemporary shrug combines texture, geometric shape, and elegance all in one—and the tassel adds a bit of whimsy to the design.

SKILL LEVEL
Intermediate

FINISHED MEASUREMENTS
50" long before connecting end to side
12" wide

YARN
2 skeins Super Bulky Yarn (CYCA 6)
2 skeins of Bulky Bouclé Yarn (CYCA 5)

SHOWN IN
Lion Brand® Homespun in Purple Haze (CYCA 5)
Lion Brand Hometown USA in Portland Wine (CYCA 6)
Lion Brand Hometown USA in Minneapolis Purple (CYCA 6)

NOTIONS (OPTIONAL)
Crochet hook for weaving in yarn ends
Needle and thread to stabilize the ends for a more finished look
An 8" piece of cardboard to wrap the yarn around to make the tassel

To Make Shrug

1. Holding two strands of the bulky and two strands of the bouclé together, cast on 8 stitches, as shown on p. 5.

2. Knit each row as shown on p. 6. Continue the process until you reach your desired length of 21 rows or approximately 50".

3. Cast off, as shown on p. 7.

Finishing

Once you have cast off just place the short end to the opposite side of the long end to make a point. Weave the tails back and forth through the knit and tie off. You can use your hands or a crochet hook.

Create a tassel by winding yarn around a piece of cardboard. Carefully slip the yarn bundle off of the cardboard and with another piece of yarn wrap and tie the bundle at one end. Cut through the loops on the other end. Attach the tassel to the point as shown in the photo above.

VARIATION Wear with the tassel in front or in back! Knit one in off-white or peach for the perfect accessory to wear for Sunday brunch, or go all out with neon yarns to really grab everyone's attention when you walk into a room.

TIP

If you don't think a cowl is for you, cast on 3 stitches instead of 5 to knit a scarf!

BLUE CORAL
COWL

This cowl is made from a yarn that invokes the peace and beauty of a coral reef. It has a three dimensional look that adds a high fashion statement to a simple shape. People will think you rule the runway!

SKILL LEVEL
Beginner

FINISHED MEASUREMENTS
36" long
10" wide

YARN
2 skeins Super Bulky
Novelty Super Bulky Yarn
(CYCA 6)

SHOWN IN
Red Heart Boutique Fizzle
in Bluefin

NOTIONS (OPTIONAL)
Needle and thread to
stabilize the ends for a
more finished look

To Make Cowl

1. Holding two strands together, cast on 5 stitches, as shown on p. 5.

Due to the long novelty strands sticking out, there is a tendency for this yarn to "stick" as you are knitting. To prevent this, you may want to wind your 2 skeins of yarn into one big ball first so that you can knit more easily.

2. Knit each row as shown on p. 6. Continue the process until you reach your desired length of 13 rows or approximately 36".

3. Cast off, as shown on p. 7.

Finishing

Once you have cast off, you will have two tails. Just place the short ends of the work together to form a cowl and link them together by weaving the tails through the knit. Finish by tying your strands into a secure knot when done.

VARIATION This yarn comes in so many fun colors, you can make one for each of your favorite outfits. Try black for an evening event, or combine two different colors like pink and purple for even more fun!

EVENING SPARKLE
TIE-ON SHRUG

This tie-on sequined shrug makes it easy to sparkle up your business attire when transitioning to an after-work event or a night on the town.

SKILL LEVEL
Beginner

FINISHED MEASUREMENTS
25" long
10" wide

YARN
2 skeins Ribbon Yarn with pre-attached sequins (CYCA 6)

SHOWN IN
Red Heart Boutique Sashay Sequins in Panda

NOTIONS (OPTIONAL)
Needle and thread to stabilize the ends for a more finished look

To Make Shrug

1. Holding two strands together, leaving an 18" tail, cast on 5 stitches, as shown on p. 5.

The sequins can get caught, so take extra care to make sure that you don't drop a stitch!

2. Knit each row as shown on p. 6. Continue the process until you reach your desired length of 15 rows or approximately 25".

3. Cast off, as shown on p. 7 leaving an 18" tail to be used as a tie.

Finishing

Once you have your shrug complete, just use the ends to tie in a bow! You may want to turn up the edges of the ties and sew them with a needle and thread for a more finished look.

VARIATION For an interesting variation, add one strand of eyelash novelty yarn and voila, even more glamour! Or tie the shrug to the side for a high fashion look.

TIP

Once you are done knitting, lay the shrug on a table and gently pull into shape to make sure you have a close to perfect rectangle. You want to make sure the shrug looks balanced once on your body!

SOFT + CUDDLY
BLANKET

This blanket is so soft and cuddly because it is made of all chenille yarns. Soft colors, soft yarn, perfect for everyone!

SKILL LEVEL
Beginner

FINISHED MEASUREMENTS
36" long
36" wide

YARN
6 skeins Super Bulky Yarn
(CYCA 6)

SHOWN IN
Bernat Baby Blanket in
Pitter Patter

NOTIONS (OPTIONAL)
Needle and thread to
stabilize the ends for a
more finished look

To Make Blanket

1. Holding all six strands together, cast on 14 stitches, as shown on p. 5.

Knitting with 6 strands of yarn at once may get a little confusing from time to time. Twisting the strands loosely together between each stitch will give you more control as you make your loops.

2. Knit each row as shown on p. 6. Continue the process until you reach your desired length of 13 rows or approximately or 36".

3. Cast off, as shown on p. 7.

Finishing

Weave in remaining ends. You can use your hands or a crochet hook. It is very important in this project to use a needle and thread or a sewing machine to do a quick tack to stabilize the ends of the yarn so your blanket doesn't unravel!

VARIATION Combine strands of different color solid chenille yarns to create your own variegated look!

TIP

This blanket is super fast to knit, but you should try to keep your tension fairly even as you knit by slightly slowing down since the stitches are so visible.

GREEN GODDESS CAPE

Go green with this one of a kind cape. Super chunky combinations of green create a warm and stylish cape for those cold evenings home or out on the town. You'll be a goddess wherever you go!

SKILL LEVEL
Beginner

FINISHED MEASUREMENTS
36" long before "wrapping"
14" wide

YARN
4 skeins Super Bulky Yarn (CYCA 6)
2 skeins of Bulky Bouclé Variegated Yarn (CYCA 5)

SHOWN IN
Lion Brand Homespun in Olive (CYCA 5)
Lion Brand Homespun in Pesto (CYCA 5)
Lion Brand Hometown USA in Lemongrass (2 skeins) (CYCA 6)
Lion Brand Hometown USA in Oklahoma City Green (CYCA 6)
Lion Brand Hometown USA in Monterey Lime (CYCA 6)

NOTIONS (OPTIONAL)
Crochet hook for weaving in yarn ends
Needle and thread to stabilize the ends for a more finished look

To Make Cape

1. Holding 6 strands together (4 strands of the super bulky and 2 strands of the bouclé), cast on 8 stitches, as shown on p. 5.

You will have a lot of the bouclé yarn left over when you finish because there is more yarn on a bouclé skein than on a bulky skein. Save it for another project or, better yet, make a second cape for your best friend!

2. Knit each row as shown on p. 6. Continue the process until you reach your desired length of 23 rows or approximately or 36".

3. Cast off, as shown on p. 7. Fold in thirds inside out.

Finishing

Once you have cast off and have your cape folded, take the yarn ends and weave into the opposite side where it lands on the cape. Repeat. You can use your hands or a crochet hook. Turn right side out. Once placed on the body, the bottom edge will spread open creating a beautiful butterfly look.

VARIATION Make a slightly wider version by casting on 10 stitches instead of 8. Any more, and the weight of the yarn may "pull" the stitches down making the cape a little saggy looking.

TIP

For an even
faster time
knitting, roll
all six skeins of
yarn into one
big ball before
beginning.

TIP

After you do the finishing of the collar, try the capelet on before connecting the center front seam so that you can decide where to stop the seam when you weave it together.

TURQUOISE FANTASY
COLLARED CAPELET

With vibrant jewel tones and super giant stitches, this collared capelet is a work of art.

SKILL LEVEL
Experienced

FINISHED MEASUREMENTS
60" long
16" wide at widest point

YARN
6 skeins Ribbon Type Yarn (CYCA 6)

SHOWN IN
Red Heart Boutique Trio in Aqueus

NOTIONS (OPTIONAL)
Crochet hook for weaving in yarn ends

Needle and thread to stabilize the ends for a more finished look

Note: Make sure you leave a 2-yard tail at cast on and cast off— if you don't you may need to take the capelet apart and start over!

To Make Collared Capelet

1. Although you are only using 4 working strands, you will need 6 skeins of ribbon yarn for this project. Divide the two remaining skeins evenly so that you have four strands, which you will tie on to your working strands when you begin to run low. Holding four strands together, cast on 20 stitches, as shown on p. 5. Leave a 2-yard tail.

2. Knit 2 rows. On your next row, K2TOG across your 20 stitches, which will leave you with 10 stitches (see p. 7 for instructions on K2TOG). Knit 1 row. On your next row, K2TOG across your 10 stitches, leaving you with 5 stitches.

3. Cast off, as shown on p. 7. Leaving the 2-yard tail mentioned in the note above.

Finishing

Once you have cast off, take the yarn end at cast off and "wrap" around the five cast off stitches creating a stand up collar effect. Weave in the end. You can use your hand or a crochet hook. Fold the capelet in half with seam in the center front. Weave in cast on tail to connect center front two rows up. Weave in end.

VARIATION Use the same pattern above using Bulky Variegated Chenille Yarn (CYCA 5), just hold double the amount of strands together.

When switching your CYCA numbers and changing to a different type of yarn, using the same pattern, you may have to buy more skeins, and/or reduce the number of strands. Try your own combinations, you can be the designer!

If you like these projects, you'll love these other fun craft booklets

DecoDen Bling
Mini decorations for phones & favorite things

Alice Fisher

DecoDen is all about bringing bling to every aspect of your life—from your sunglasses to your cellphone to everything in between! Best of all, the decadent sparkle of this hot decorating technique is just a few simple techniques away. From phone cases to wall clocks to picture frames and more, the 20 recipes in this booklet will show you exactly what you need to glam up your day.

32 pages, product #078046, $9.95 U.S.

Bungee Band Bracelets & More
12 projects to make with bungee band & paracord

Vera Vandenbosch

Bungee cord is no longer just a tool—now available in a wide variety of colors and thicknesses, it's the perfect material for you to create beautiful bracelets and necklaces. The 12 projects in this booklet will show you exactly how to transform this stretchy material into runway-worthy designs for you to wear and show off.

32 pages, product #078048, $9.95 U.S.

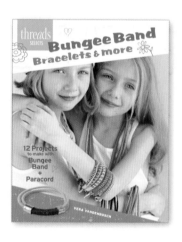

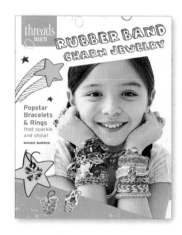

Rubber Band Charm Jewelry
popstar bracelets & rings that sparkle and shine

Maggie Marron

This booklet offers 15 great jewelry projects to make on or off of your loom—rings, bracelets, anklets, and even charms made out of nothing but rubber bands! Spice up your day the popstar way and let loose with these celebrity-inspired accessories. Learn how to make fishtails, starbursts, tulips, and so much more as you grab a little piece of the spotlight for yourself!

32 pages, product #078047, $9.95 U.S.

Shop for these and other great craft books and booklets online: www.tauntonstore.com

Simply search by product number or call 800-888-8286, use code MX800126

Call Monday-Friday 9AM - 9PM EST and Saturday 9AM - 5PM EST • International customers, call 203-702-2204